Why I'm Grateful for You

1

I'm grateful we're such

____.

2

I'm always grateful to get your advice on

____.

3

I'm grateful that you always make me feel

______________________________,

even when

______________________________.

4

I'm grateful that you never make me feel

____,

even when

____.

5

I'm forever grateful that you
introduced me to

____.

6

I'm grateful for how you make
the world a more

____

place.

7

The way you say,

"____"

always makes me laugh.

8

I'd be so grateful if you got all the

____

you deserve. (And then some.)

9

If you were an Olympic sport,

you'd be

____.

10

Thanks again for the time

you helped me

____.

11

I'm super grateful for the way you make

____.

12

Remembering the time we

____

fills me with

______________________________.

13

You deserve a lifetime supply of

____

and

____!

14

I'm grateful I get to hear all your

____

stories about

____.

15

You prove it's possible to be

____

and

____.

16

I'm eternally grateful for every time you

____.

17

I feel so grateful that I get to watch you

______________________________________.

18

You win the Best

____

Ever Award!

19

I'm so grateful we got to

____

that one time.

20

I'm grateful for your beautiful

____.

21

I’m super grateful for the

____

you gave me.

22

When I see

____,

it always reminds me of you.

23

I'm grateful that we both enjoy

____

so much.

24

I'm grateful that we both dislike

____

so much!

25

I'm grateful for the sound of your

____.

26

I think everyone would be grateful
if you were in charge of

______________________________________.

27

I'm grateful that you always know what to

____

when

____.

28

I'm grateful for the way you

____

every day.

29

Thank you for all the times you've listened to me

____.

30

I'm grateful for the time you told me

____.

31

I'd be grateful to have even an ounce of your

____.

32

I’m grateful to call you

____.

33

You're my role model for

____.

34

Thank you for letting me borrow your

_______________________________________.

35

I'm grateful that you always see the

____

in me.

36

I'm so grateful that you tolerate my

____!

37

Thank you for never giving up on

____.

38

If you ever decided to

____,

I'd be really, really grateful!

39

I'm so grateful for the time you took me

____.

40

I'm grateful you have such

____

taste in

____.

41

I'm grateful for how you take care of

____.

42

I hope you know how grateful
everyone is for your

____.

43

Thank you for being more

____

than most people.

44

Thank you for being less

____

than most people.

45

If you were a superhero,

your superpower would be

____.

46

I feel grateful to see how

happy you are when

____.

47

I’m thankful that you’re always up for

____.

48

I really depend on your

____.

49

I'm so grateful for the way you sing

____.

50

I'm so

____

you came into my life.

I’m So Grateful for You!

Fill in the *Love*.®

Created, published, and distributed by Knock Knock
11111 Jefferson Blvd. #5167
Culver City, CA 90231
knockknockstuff.com
Knock Knock is a registered trademark of Knock Knock LLC
Fill in the Love is a registered trademark of Knock Knock LLC

ISBN: 978-168349002-9
UPC: 825703-50257-2

12

#fillinthelove